GOO PICCADILLY

FROM HOME FRONT TO WESTERN FRONT

Exhibition at London Transport Museum
May 2014 – March 2015

Published in 2014 by
London Transport Museum
Covent Garden Piazza
London WC2E 7BB
Tel +44 (0)20 7379 6344

Copyright © London Transport Museum 2014

Designed by LTM Design

ISBN 978-1-871829-21-1

ltmuseum.co.uk
Registered charity number 1123122

london
transport
museum

ACKNOWLEDGEMENTS

London Transport Museum would like to thank all the institutions and individuals who have contributed images and objects for this exhibition and publication. A particular thanks also to those who helped with the original research and development of the exhibition: David Bownes, former Head Curator LTM, David Lawrence, Research Fellow, LTM and Professor Jerry White, author of *Zeppelin Nights: London in the First World War*.

GOODBYE PICCADILLY
FROM HOME FRONT TO WESTERN FRONT

Women conductors receive
training on a B-type bus, 1916
1998/91203

FOREWORD

The cheering crowds that thronged London's Whitehall, Trafalgar Square and the Strand to welcome the declaration of war on Germany at midnight on 4th August 1914, expected the conflict to be short and victorious. The bus drivers whose buses were stuck in amongst the crowds, and from which revellers had a grandstand view of the celebrations, had little idea that they might find both themselves and their buses on the Western Front within a matter of weeks. Certainly, the duration and profound effect of war on the London of 1914 could hardly have been anticipated. Neither could the bus drivers know the realities of loss and destruction they would witness, and write to their loved ones about.

Total, or world war, was a creation of the 1914-18 conflict. London was protected by the English Channel from the ruinous conjunction of home and fighting visited upon countless French and Belgian towns and cities. However, the War was on its doorstep, and the Capital became a centre of wartime operations which brought civilians and the armed services into common cause. London was a hive of activity for five years, its railway and Underground stations thronged with soldiers and sailors departing for the front or returning home on leave, or arriving wounded via Waterloo or Victoria, destined for the Capital's many hospitals. Munitions were manufactured around the Capital – especially in the East End – and transported with food and animal fodder, guns and equipment, horses, vehicles, and medical supplies, to France.

The face of the city was changed too, and not only from being dominated by men in uniform: allotments were dug in Hyde Park, searchlights combed the night skies as the city was bombed from the air for the first time and subjected to blackout regulations, the sizeable German community was set upon by mobs, U-boat attacks led to food shortages and rationing, while theatres and the new medium of film flourished.

The emancipation of women had been a major social issue in the years before the War. As the services consumed more and more men, they had to be replaced. Women, many of whom had been hidden away as domestic servants, took up male roles for the first time, and were especially visible as bus conductors, platform staff, railway guards, cleaners and lift attendants.

Over a thousand London buses, about a third of the city's bus fleet, were requisitioned and sent to France, accompanied by their drivers into the Army Service Corps. A touch of London was brought to the fighting front, as convoys of buses, initially with their colourful paintwork, adverts and route boards intact, carried troops towards the fighting lines and brought the wounded out. A handful of buses returned to service on the Capital's streets after the War, and one bus, B43, was presented to George V and rechristened 'Ole Bill' after Bruce Bairnsfather's cartoon character. Veteran bus drivers were the only civilians to march in the first Remembrance Sunday parade, accompanied by 'Ole Bill' as a mobile memorial to the busmen's contribution to the war effort.

Post war London was much changed by war; it had lost many of its men, was wracked by the influenza epidemic of 1918, and had its economy disrupted by four years of battle. Transport struggled to return to normal with makeshift khaki-coloured lorry buses drafted onto the Capital's streets. Women lost their transport jobs, but 8.4 million of them gained the vote in 1918 and all women over 21 could vote from 1928. Memorials to the fallen were placed in London's bus garages, on railway stations and in every parish church.

The music hall song *It's a long way to Tipperary*, written in 1912, was popularized by Irish troops as they marched across northern France in August 1914, when they cheered themselves by singing the lyrics *'Goodbye Piccadilly, Farewell Leicester Square!'* Our exhibition brings to the light the London which went to war in 1914 and the experience of civilian Londoners, bus drivers in France, female conductors on the platforms of their buses and those caught up in air raids on the city. 'Goodbye Piccadilly' symbolizes the vanished hopes of the generation of Londoners caught up in the Great War, the lost city of the warm summer of 1914 and the yearning for home as Londoners marched into the whirlwind of total war. Finally, the exhibition returns us to peacetime London, and the part our transport system played in post-war recovery.

Sam Mullins
Director, London Transport Museum

PICCADILLY · TUBE

The First World War changed London and Londoners forever. For the drivers who took their buses to the Western Front and for their families and friends left behind, it meant facing new challenges at work and new ways of life.

Our title comes from the song 'It's a Long Way to Tipperary'. Written in 1912, it was popularised by Irish troops as they marched through northern France in August 1914. It soon became popular across the British Army and is now one of the best remembered songs from the First World War.

It's a long way to Tipperary
It's a long way to go
It's a long way to Tipperary
To the sweetest girl I know
GOODBYE PICCADILLY
Farewell Leicester Square
It's a long, long way to Tipperary
But my heart's right there

MODERN LONDON TAKES SHAPE

In 1900 London was a great industrial, political and commercial city at the heart of an empire covering a quarter of the Earth. London created enormous wealth and was modernising at a rapid pace.

New technology, including electric tube railways and motorised transport, had transformed the city in the years before 1914. Faster and cheaper modes of transport gave access to new forms of entertainment, luxurious department stores and grand hotels. But despite these advances, there were still many inequalities, with women still denied the vote and considerable urban poverty.

Piccadilly Circus, busy with horse-drawn cabs and buses, 1900
2004/18480

THE ROAD TO PLEASURE

As London grew, transport companies competed to promote services to new shopping districts, theatres, cinemas, sporting events and exhibitions. Films grew in popularity and sophistication with new purpose-built venues. Film stars became famous and individual actors were credited on screen for the first time. Cinemas also began weekly newsreel screenings showing events from around the world.

Gentle persuasion

Posters like these served an important commercial purpose. Off-peak travel to the growing entertainment and shopping districts of West London was a valuable source of income for all transport companies.

Theatres and halls by tram – alight at Hammersmith Broadway, Charles Sharland, 1913
1983/4/231

The most convenient way to the shops – by Underground, artist unknown, 1909
1983/4/8111

Chelsea v Arsenal, artist unknown, 1913
2004/19753

Whatever degree of pleasure you may seek, artist unknown, 1912
2000/2198

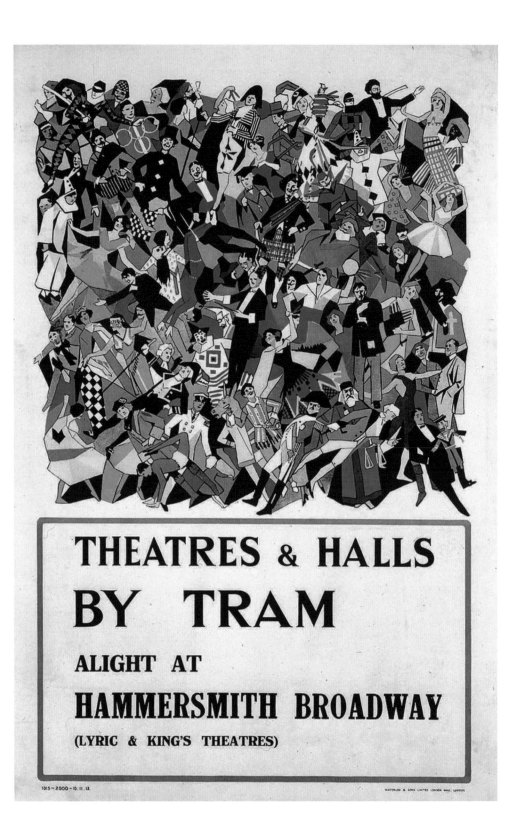

THEATRES & HALLS BY TRAM
ALIGHT AT HAMMERSMITH BROADWAY
(LYRIC & KING'S THEATRES)

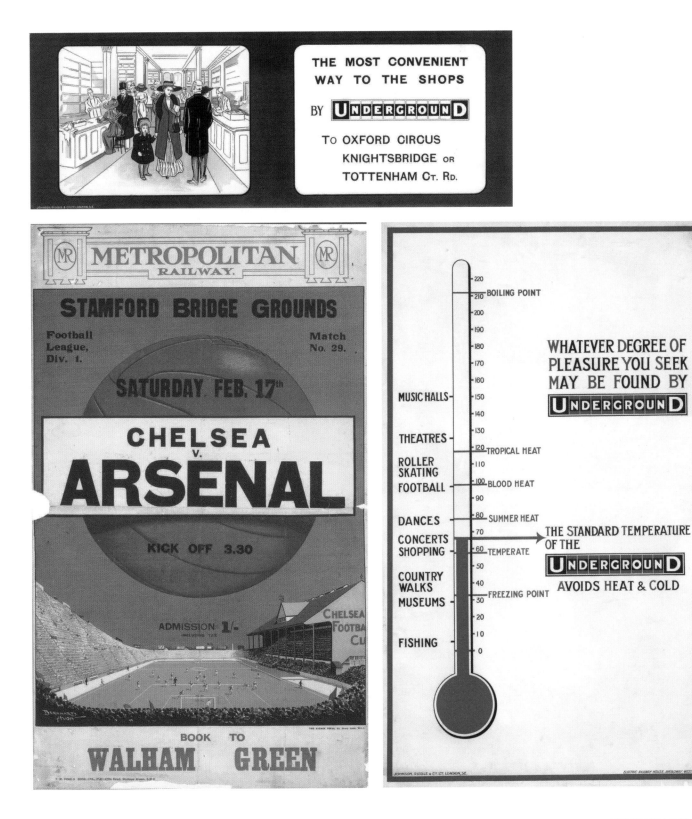

Premonitions

With hindsight, posters like these seem to anticipate the concerns of the coming war. Walter Spradbery's quiet country road appears especially poignant since hundreds of London buses and their drivers would soon be swapping the 'fresh air and sunshine' of an idealised England for the mud and khaki of Belgium and France.

Territorial review, Charles Sharland, 1913
1983/4/290

The open road, fresh air and sunshine,
Walter Spradbery, 1914
1983/4/555

November   Fifteen Cents

PHOTOPLAY

MAGAZINE

1914

"GROWING UP WITH THE MOVIES" BY FLORENCE LAWRENCE

AND ANOTHER JESSE LASKY NOVELETTE

The Biograph Girl

Film actors were not individually credited on screen before 1910. The first person to have this honour was the Canadian Florence Lawrence. She is considered cinema's first star, although originally billed only as 'The Biograph Girl' after the studio she worked for.

archive.org

The Picturedome, East Finchley, 1912

London already had 265 cinemas in 1911, most converted from other uses. The Picturedome was one of London's earliest purpose-built cinemas and opened its doors in 1910. Now known as the Phoenix, it is still showing films today.

Courtesy of the Phoenix Cinema

FROM COMPETITION TO INTEGRATION

London's transport networks grew rapidly in the decade before the First World War. Bus and railway companies competed for customers on busy commuter routes and local councils set up their own electric tram services. In 1910, the London General Omnibus Company (LGOC) introduced the first reliable motor bus, the B-type. As transport companies merged, the pooling of resources led to increased efficiency. Design contributed to the sense of an integrated network.

B is best

Motorised buses had been operating in London since 1899, but early vehicles were unreliable and only produced in small numbers. Between 1908 and 1910 London's largest bus company, the LGOC, developed the B-type. It was a great success: nearly 2,500 were in service by 1914.

LGOC bus route map, 1911
2010/2884

Accidents, Tony Sarg, 1913
1983/4/223

New B-type buses at Cricklewood garage, north-west London, 1911
1998/84482

One of a range of experimental safety features for the B-type is tested on a dummy, Walthamstow, December 1912
2013/9818

District Railway electric trains

District Railway trains were hauled by steam locomotives for nearly 40 years before the line was electrified in 1905. The new electric American-style trains must have seemed very futuristic in the grimy tunnels of the Victorian underground.

Artist unknown, 1908
1983/4/1

Birth of a brand

Three new tube railways opened in 1906-7, and are known to us now as the Piccadilly, Bakerloo and Northern lines. They had common ownership and a unified look, but the railways were initially promoted separately.
The introduction of the umbrella brand 'UndergrounD' and the roundel symbol in 1908, created the idea of a network with a shared identity.

Watercolour of Oxford Circus station, signed by the architect Leslie Green, 1906
1994/557

Pocket Underground map, 1915
2010/2879

WEALTH, POVERTY AND UNREST

Economic prosperity and technological advances were changing London in the 1900s. The middle classes started to move out to new railway suburbs, but many Londoners still lived in poverty in slums, without adequate education or health care. Inequality between the rich and poor increased, as social improvements lagged behind technological change. Only 30% of the population had the vote.

Slum dwellers in Matthew Parker Street, a short walk from the Houses of Parliament, 1904
1999/2728

The road to pleasure, artist unknown, 1909
1983/4/8105

The suffragettes

The struggle for women's equality and voting rights was fought by a range of groups. Most militant was the Women's Social and Political Union, whose members became known as the 'suffragettes'. They used demonstrations as well as criminal damage, hunger strikes and arson to raise awareness of their cause. Over 1,000 women were imprisoned between 1905 and 1914.

Women's Coronation Procession leaflet, 1911
Museum of London

VOTES FOR WOMEN

Women's Coronation

PROCESSION

(Five miles long).

Saturday, June 17th,

START 5.30 P.M.

Route via:—TRAFALGAR SQUARE, PALL MALL, PICCADILLY, KNIGHTSBRIDGE.

70 BANDS!
1,000 BANNERS!

THE PROCESSION will march to Kensington, where great meetings in the ROYAL ALBERT HALL and in the EMPRESS ROOMS will be held by the Women's Social and Political Union, at 8.30 p.m., in support of the Woman Suffrage Bill.

Speakers:
Mrs. PANKHURST, Mrs. PETHICK LAWRENCE, Miss VIDA GOLDSTEIN, Miss CHRISTABEL PANKHURST, and others.

Tickets for the Meeting in the EMPRESS ROOMS for Numbered and Reserved Seats, price 2s. 6d. and 1s., can be obtained from The Ticket Secretary, W.S.P.U., 4, Clements Inn, W.C.

For all further plans and particulars read the weekly newspaper VOTES FOR WOMEN. (Price One Penny.) It can be obtained at all newsagents and bookstalls.

Printed by St. Clements Press, Limited, Portugal Street, Kingsway, London, W.C.

The Great Unrest

The period of widespread industrial action and disorder up to 1914 was known as the 'Great Unrest'. Dockers and transport workers were at the forefront in London, but other groups, including the Metropolitan Police, went on strike during this turbulent period.

Men from the Thomas Tilling bus company, on strike for recognition of the Union of Licensed Vehicle Workers, September 1913
Getty Images

Banner celebrating the success of the of the 1913 Union of Licensed Vehicle Workers strike, 1913
People's History Museum

GREAT BRITAIN DECLARES WAR ON GERMANY

DECLARATION LAST NIGHT AFTER 'UNSATISFACTORY REPLY' TO BRITISH ULTIMATUM THAT BELGIUM MUST BE KEPT NEUTRAL

From the 1880s, rising tensions in Europe led to the creation of two major alliances: the Triple Alliance of Germany, Austria-Hungary and Italy, and the Triple Entente of France, Russia and Great Britain. A naval arms race between competing European empires in the early 1900s pushed forward military technology. On 28 June 1914, Archduke Franz Ferdinand of Austria and his wife were assassinated by Serb nationalists in Sarajevo, Bosnia. This act sparked a chain of events that escalated into the outbreak of war across Europe.

OVER BY CHRISTMAS

When Britain declared war on Germany on
4 August 1914, crowds of Londoners celebrated
in the streets. Most believed that Britain would
win quickly and the fighting would be 'over by
Christmas'. However, few people could predict
what modern, mechanised warfare would involve.
Within hours, long-prepared military plans kicked in
and London became an operational centre for war
and the mass movement of troops.

*'For more than four hours the
singing and cheering of the crowd
was maintained without a break.'*

THE TIMES REPORTING ON THE OUTBREAK OF WAR,
5 AUGUST 1914

KEY

CENTRAL POWERS
*Italy was allied to the Central Powers but
refused to join the war in August 1914

ALLIED NATIONS

NEUTRAL

MOBILISING FOR WAR

Although the British Army had few motor vehicles of its own in 1914, it had recognised some years previously that motor transport would be essential in modern warfare. In 1912, the Government Subsidy Scheme assessed the suitability of commercial motor vehicles for military service. In the event of war, the government agreed to pay civilian businesses in return for taking over their vans, lorries and buses.

Days before war began, 30 buses from the London General Omnibus Company (LGOC) were requisitioned. They were hurriedly converted into ambulances and dispatched to the front line. Soon, hundreds of drivers and buses were mobilised to transport troops and supplies.

'Waiting for war', *The Graphic*, 8 August 1914

On 4 August, Britain offered an ultimatum to Germany, demanding the removal of German troops from Belgium by midnight. Many Britons were shocked by the invasion of neutral Belgium and were supportive of British intervention. Over several tense hours, Londoners gathered on Whitehall awaiting news.

A steady stream of foreign ambassadors visited Downing Street. By midnight, news from Germany was 'unsatisfactory' and war was declared. The assembled crowds cheered the news.

2013/8056

WAITING FOR WAR: THE CROWD IN WHITEHALL ON TUESDAY NIGHT

Enormous crowds gathered in Whitehall on Tuesday night and waited eagerly for news of how Germany had received our ultimatum. It became known shortly before midnight that we had declared war at 11 o'clock, and when midnight struck an enormous shout went up, for 11 p.m. London time is midnight in Berlin. The crowd waited for the Ministers to leave Downing Street. Mr. Churchill had a thrilling reception. The German Ambassador, who looked haggard, was in no way molested as he motored home.

AN IMPRESSION BY TORRANCE STEPHENSON

A B-type bus passing a unit of cavalry
on Fleet Street, central London, 1914
1998/86761

'We passed an enormous
detachment of recruits
marching over Waterloo
Bridge… We soon got used to
that sort of thing though, there
were soldiers everywhere.'

WINIFRED TOWER, A LONDONER RETURNING
FROM HOLIDAY, 15 OCTOBER 1914

LGOC buses converted to ambulances with
LGOC drivers and Royal Navy personnel, 1914
1998/36874

**Toyland, mobilizing for Christmas
Tony Sarg, 1914**

For Christmas 1914, Tony Sarg updated
his 1913 Toyland poster. The main image
remained the same but at the bottom
toy soldiers, horses and a nurse are
shown 'mobilising'. By the time this
poster was issued, it was clear that the
war would not be 'over by Christmas'.

1983/4/335

In Toyland, Tony Sarg, 1913
1983/4/336

*'My grandmother… took from
us all our toys that were made in
Germany, amongst them a camel
of which I was very fond.'*

ELIZABETH OWEN, AGED 7 IN 1914, INTERVIEWED
BY THE IMPERIAL WAR MUSEUM IN 1963

WILLING MEN MAKE HAPPY FIGHTERS

Despite its naval strength, Britain's army of 500,000 trained men, including reservists, compared unfavourably with the nearly four million men mobilised by Germany. On 6 August 1914, Lord Kitchener, the British Secretary of War, called for 100,000 civilians to join up. Recruitment messages were all over London.

Although London's transport companies were independent of government, they joined in the recruitment drive with their own poster campaigns. Transport staff volunteered in their thousands, sometimes taking on military roles related to their civilian jobs such as driving buses or working as mechanics.

Images of war

Like many businesses, the Underground Group 'did its bit' for the war effort. Commercial Manager, Frank Pick, was one of Britain's most adventurous poster commissioners. He was dissatisfied with the government-issued recruitment posters, seeing them as crude and potentially counter-productive, so he commissioned the Underground's own.

Two of Pick's 1914 commissions were from Frank Brangwyn and Gerald Spencer Pryse who both created dramatic, graphic representations of war to boost recruitment.

Both artists designed posters that showed the cost to civillians the invasion of Belgium.

War – to arms citizens of the Empire!!
Frank William Brangwyn, 1914
1983/4/672

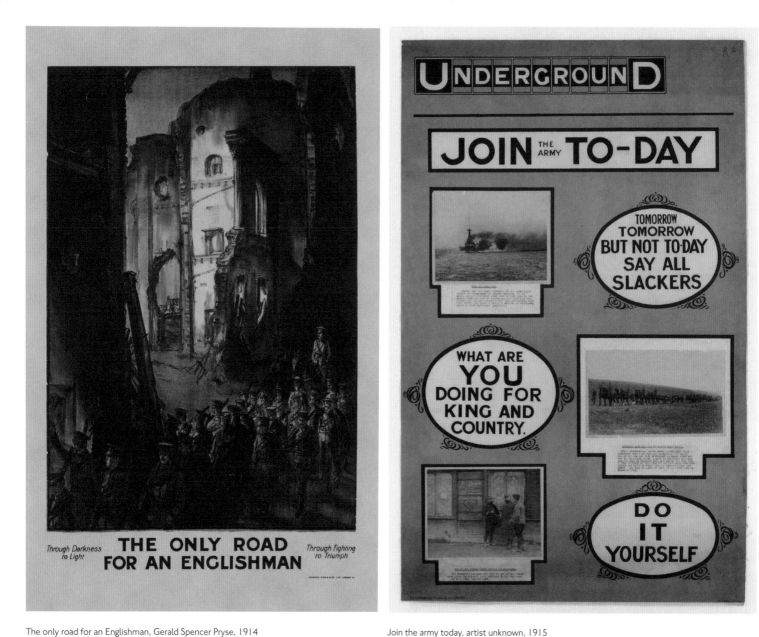

The only road for an Englishman, Gerald Spencer Pryse, 1914
1995/541

Join the army today, artist unknown, 1915
1983/4/577

'It'll be over by Christmas… you've got to get out
soon otherwise you won't see anything.'

BILL HAIN, WHO VOLUNTEERED IN THE EARLY DAYS OF THE WAR,
SPEAKING TO THE IMPERIAL WAR MUSEUM IN THE 1960S

A B-type bus carries City of London Police volunteers to a recruiting station, 1914 1998/36810

WILLING MEN MAKE HAPPY FIGHTERS

Let us go to the War of our own
free-will and not wait till we must

ENLIST AT ONCE.   100,000 WANTED

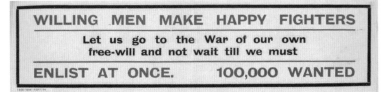

A CALL TO ARMS

Are you between 19 and 35?
Are you physically fit?
Are you without home ties?

THEN YOU ARE WANTED AT THE WAR

ENGLAND v GERMANY.

SIGN ON AT ONCE FOR THE
GRAND INTERNATIONAL FINAL.

EVERY MAN COUNTS.

Willing men make happy fighters, 1914
1983/4/8160

A call to arms, 1914
1983/4/8158

England v Germany, 1915
1983/4/8154

WAR ON OUR DOORSTEPS

The First World War was the first mechanised conflict and ordinary Londoners found themselves on the front line for the first time. There were bombing attacks from German airships and aeroplanes, U-Boat attacks on shipping and blockades of ports, resulting in food shortages. All these brought the war to London's doorstep.

The war touched everyone in London, as industries came under government control. The close proximity of the fighting in Northern France meant that troops on leave could make it home with relative ease. As more men joined up, patterns of social and working lives changed for those left behind.

Bus conductors being fitted
with their new uniforms, 1916
1998/85837

WOMEN'S WAR WORK

With so many men away fighting, women were called upon to sustain the war effort at home. They took on skilled and physical tasks that had previously always been regarded as 'men's work'.

Employment was on a temporary basis while the men were away, and these pioneers received a mixed response as society reacted to seeing women in new roles.

Such an unprecedented mobilisation of female labour offered thousands of women greater responsibility and financial independence. Equally importantly, it showed that they were as capable as any man.

LONDON GENERAL OMNIBUS COMPANY, L.T.D.

WANTED

WOMEN CONDUCTORS

HEIGHT MUST NOT BE LESS THAN 5 FEET AGE BETWEEN 21 AND 35

APPLY BETWEEN 10.0 A.M. AND 1.0 P.M.
ON WEEKDAYS (SATURDAYS EXCEPTED)

THE SUPERINTENDENT OF EMPLOYMENT,
L.G.O. CO'S. TRAINING SCHOOL,
MILMAN'S STREET,
S.W.

London General Omnibus Company recruitment poster for female bus conductors, 1916
In March 1916 when the LGOC published this poster, 20,000 women applied. The LGOC went on to employ over 3,500 women, sometimes called 'conductorettes', over the next three years.

2003/24157 part 24

Kitted out
New conductors were given a uniform, a ticket machine and a licence badge issued by the Metropolitan Police. Heavy serge overcoats were supplied for the winter months, but proved cumbersome on hot and overcrowded buses. In summer the 'conductorettes' had the option of wearing a white jacket and straw hat.

Leather lace-up gaiters were worn over boots and came up to the knee. Bus conductor Florence Cordell described putting these on first thing in the morning as a 'blinking nuisance!'

LGOC female bus conductor uniform, 1916-19
2002/2025

Metropolitan Railway register of female employees, Volume one, 1915-19

A close eye was kept on female workers employed by the Metropolitan Railway and any misdemeanours were recorded in a staff register. The records reveal women being cautioned for lateness, or being absent after seeing off soldier sons and brothers returning to France. More seriously, 'lady booking clerk' Helena Warwick was summarily discharged for being 'under influence of drink whilst on duty'.

In another incident, Lily Hobbs was demoted from liftwoman to porteress for 'allowing a police constable to accompany her whilst operating the lift'. The entry states 'considerable scandal caused at Essex Road by this, but Mrs Hobbs' husband explained that the constable was a friend of his, in whom he had perfect confidence'.

2007/11017

Florence Cordell, 1916, LGOC bus conductor
1998/84340

Anne Parker, 1916, LGOC bus conductor
1998/83712

A Metropolitan Railway guard at Neasden station, north-west London, 1917

This guard is giving the 'all clear' signal to the driver. She would then board the train as it left the station. For safety reasons, the skirts were shorter than usual. The uniform also included knee-length knickers which were tucked into the boots, preventing any flesh from being revealed.

1998/84028

Painters at Hammersmith station, west London, c1917

The sight of women in trousers was new and shocking, but the demands of work made long skirts impractical. Instead, the women here are wearing long jackets over their trousers, which were supposed to protect their modesty.

1998/37266

An LGOC female worker repairs the rear axle of a bus, c1917
2003/8031

Work, work, work

Before becoming a bus conductor, applicants had to pass a medical examination and an intelligence test. After two weeks of training, each woman sat a final examination.

Nearly half of the women conductors of 1916 had previously worked in domestic service. Such work could be ill-paid and monotonous and involved living in the employer's home. By comparison, a conductor had higher wages and greater personal freedom.

But the hours were still long. Conductors worked seven days a week, with only every third Sunday off. Any holiday taken was unpaid. Women were also only employed on a temporary basis.

Photographs from an album called 'Woman conductors: A brief history, on the occasion of the two thousandth appointment', March – December 1916
2005/13405

'… there was a canteen upstairs…and as we walked in, all these old chaps looked at us and said "Oh my Lor'… All brand new and never been unwrapped!"'

FLORENCE CORDELL, LGOC BUS CONDUCTOR, INTERVIEWED BY LONDON TRANSPORT MUSEUM IN 1985

ELIZA COMES — TO STAY P

Another effect of the war—the A.G.M. decided to admit women members.

Equal pay for equal work

Many working men feared that the new women's workforce would be used by employers as a cheap source of labour, which in turn would drive down men's wages. To avoid this, trade unionists resolved to support equal pay for female workers, but capped at the starting rate.

Spontaneous strikes stopped transport in London during August 1918 as women workers on buses, trams and the Underground successfully demanded the war bonus, which until then had only been paid to men.

National Union of Railwaymen, Railway Review, July 1915
Modern Records Centre

Driver and female conductor on B-type bus, c1917
1998/252412

A KHAKI 'BUS-CONDUCTRESS : IN HER NEW AND BECOMING UNIFORM.

The woman-conductor is proving so satisfactory a substitute for men who have answered the call to serve their country, and are now at the front, or in military training, or doing some sort of war-work, that it looks as though she were come to stay. Alert, helpful to unaccustomed travellers, she well becomes her smart new khaki uniform, and is winning good opinions and good wishes.—[*Photo. by Photopress.*]

Mixed messages

'Conductorettes' were a prominent part of the war effort, and most people respected female transport workers as capable and conscientors. For some though, the novelty of women transport workers was a source of amusement and innuendo.

Article from Illustrated War News, 5 April 1916
2013/12087

Postcard of a bus conductor, c1916
2009/8171

… they had girls on the railway… and then they had girls on the trams and I thought… I wish they had them on the buses, I'd love to scoot along the road!

ANNE PARKER, LGOC BUS CONDUCTOR, INTERVIEWED BY LONDON TRANSPORT MUSEUM IN 1990

FRED SPURGIN

IF YOU WANT TO GET OFF "RING" THE BELLE.

"Doing her Bit"

FARES PLEASE.

Doing her bit – fares please, c1917
At first glance this postcard appears innocent enough, but it could be interpreted as mocking female bus conductors. Suffragettes were also sometimes depicted as children in order to undermine their struggle for equality.

2013/8058

From porter to ticket inspector

When the new Maida Vale Underground station opened on 6 June 1915, it was staffed entirely by women. The range of women's roles during the war was celebrated in a set of lithographs published by the Underground Group in 1918.

Photograph of ticket inspector at Maida Vale station, c1915
1998/39279

War Work – Playing the game, (Gatewoman), AS Hartrick, 1918
1985/2/6

Railway women

Before the war, women worked for the railways but usually in roles with lower status and pay such as cleaning and catering. However, by the spring of 1915 it became necessary to employ women, referred to as 'substitutes,' in traditional male roles. On the London Underground and Metropolitan Railway women worked as ticket inspectors, booking clerks, porters, lift attendants, cleaners, painters and guards.

Many men felt that women were incapable of taking on such important duties, particularly those of the guard, responsible for the safety of passengers and the train. The one role women were not allowed to fill was that of train driver. This was reserved for men until the first female Tube train driver was employed in 1978.

Metropolitan Railway guards at Neasden station, north-west London, 1917
2002/8707

LONDON UNDER ATTACK

From the early days of the war, fear of aerial bombardment loomed large over London. The government was aware of the threat posed by Germany's airships, the most famous being the 'Zeppelins', named after their inventor Count Ferdinand von Zeppelin. Searchlights and basic air defences were installed and from 1 September 1914, nightly blackouts were enforced to prevent detection of targets from the air. On 31 May 1915, a Zeppelin dropped the first bomb on the capital, on Stoke Newington in north-east London.

The Theatre-land attack

On 13 October 1915, London suffered its fifth Zeppelin attack. It was known as the 'Theatre-land' attack as the first bombs landed on the West End during the evening theatre interval. The very first bomb of the night was dropped about 100 metres from London Transport Museum in Covent Garden. During the raid, a bomb hit a bus in Kingsway, killing both the driver, Mr Tarrant and conductor, Mr Rogers.

Bomb damage to the Strand Theatre, central London, 13 October 1915
2014/1298

Bus licence plate with shrapnel damage, from raid on 13 October 1915
On loan from the Metropolitan Police Heritage Centre

Postcard showing funeral of driver Tarrant and conductor Rogers in Clapton, east London, 20 October 1915
2004/9277

Searchlights at Hyde Park
Corner, September 1914
2013/12352

Aerial map of London showing
Zeppelin raids, 1915–1917
2013/8357

Passengers are requested to keep
the blinds drawn at night, 1915
2003/24294

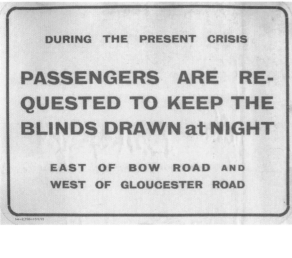

DURING THE PRESENT CRISIS

PASSENGERS ARE RE-QUESTED TO KEEP THE BLINDS DRAWN at NIGHT

EAST OF BOW ROAD AND
WEST OF GLOUCESTER ROAD

*'I remember running… to Piccadilly Circus
Tube station and going down those
hundreds of stairs, round and round… when
I got there we were all crowded, nothing but
bodies lying around the place.'*

JESSIE MATTHEWS, BRITISH ACTRESS, ON HER EXPERIENCES
OF SHELTERING IN THE UNDERGROUND AS A CHILD

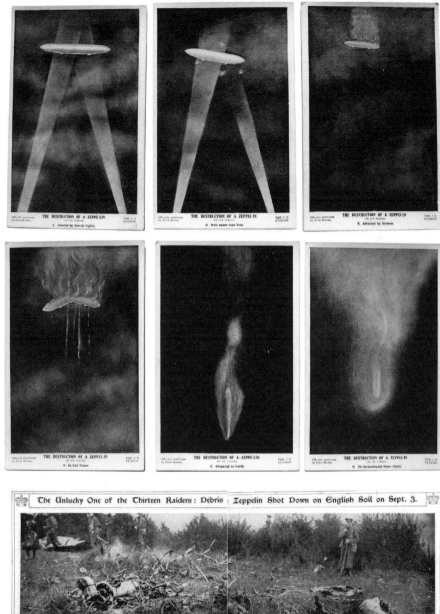

'It looked like a big silver cigar in the sky and it fascinated me beyond everything… it was like an express train over your head, it was an incredible noise that it made.'

AGNES MACALISTER, GOLDERS GREEN, INTERVIEWED BY THE IMPERIAL WAR MUSEUM IN THE 1960s

Zeppelins shot down

From February 1916, London saw an increase in searchlights, anti-aircraft guns and observation posts. Better training and technical advances meant that more pilots and aircraft were able to operate at night.

On 3 September 1916, the British public received a huge morale boost when 2nd Lieutenant William Leefe Robinson became the first pilot to shoot down an airship over British soil.

Thousands of Londoners witnessed the attack and cheered as the Zeppelin was brought down. Robinson was awarded the Victoria Cross for bravery.

Six postcards showing the Destruction of a Zeppelin, 1917
2013/11107

In the leash of the lights, *The War Illustrated*, 15 April 1916
2013/8568

The unlucky one of the thirteen raiders, *Illustrated War News*, September 1916
2013/12275

Zeppelin air raid damage to a house in Ramsgate, Kent, May 1915

Londoners had become familiar with images of air raid damage elsewhere in the country before coming under direct attack themselves. Attacks on Britain began in January 1915, but it was not until May that the German leader Kaiser Wilhelm II, who had close ties to the British royal family, allowed the Capital to be targeted.

2013/12266

The threat intensifies

On 13 June 1917, London suffered its most devastating air raid of the war, a surprise attack in broad daylight by one of Germany's new, twin-engine 'Gotha' aeroplanes, which could fly higher than most British planes.

The raid killed over 150 people, including 18 children at a school in Poplar, east London. Another attack, on 29 September 1917, was London's first glimpse of the 'Giant' bombers. They had nearly double the Gotha's wingspan and were able to carry even more bombs. The 'Harvest Moon raids' of September and October 1917 saw five nights of bombing. Terrified Londoners sought shelter in the Underground as well as in the Blackwall and Rotherhithe tunnels.

Raid by German aeroplanes over London, 7 July 1917
2013/8319

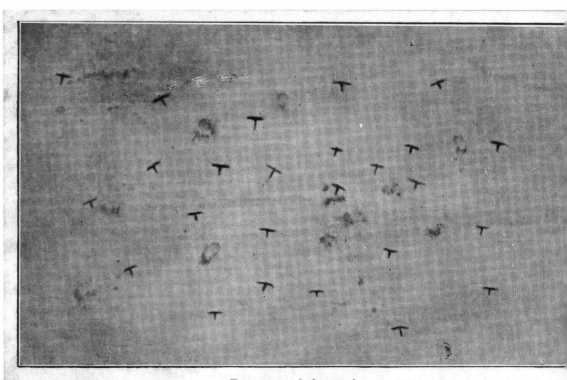

From an actual photograph.
Raid by German Aeroplanes over London on the morning of 7th July, 1917. NOTE SHELLS BURSTING.

The Underworld Walter Bayes, 1918

This is one of very few images of Londoners sheltering on the Underground during the First World War. It shows a diverse range of people seeking refuge at Elephant & Castle station. Up to 300,000 people sheltered in the Underground during air raids.

© IWM London

Damage caused by a Gotha air raid, Victoria Embankment, 4 September 1917
© IWM London

Damaged section of high tension cable from Minories Junction, Metropolitan Railway, 1917
1995/2644

TRANSPORT ADAPTS

Maintaining transport networks during wartime was crucially important, as London was the centre of war operations.

London's transport kept moving despite air raids and shortages of labour, vehicles and fuel. Services were stretched by a growing population of war workers. As demand increased, and queues at bus stops and stations lengthened, safety and etiquette campaigns helped to ease the extra pressure on services. Standing on the lower deck of a bus was allowed for the first time.

Trade unions, conscription and reserved occupations

Transport staff held divided views about the war. Many volunteered to fight, but labour and union newspapers opposed conscription well before it was introduced in 1916. Some skilled staff who might otherwise have joined up were kept back by their employers for essential war work. Badges and armbands issued from December 1914 signified work of national importance to help prevent accusations of cowardice.

Railway Service lapel badge, 1914
1999/31983

Underground staff with 'War Service' armbands, c1915
1998/36535

Cartoon, Daily Herald, January 1916
Modern Records Centre

THE MAN BEHIND CONSCRIPTION
" Why these unfounded working-class suspicions of Conscription? "—" National Service " plaint.

War production

In the spring of 1915, the country was shocked to discover that the British army was running perilously short of artillery shells. Only then did the government recognise that the whole economy would have to be geared for war if Britain and her Allies were to win. Many companies converted factories to war work, including the LGOC Chiswick Works in west London.

Shell production at Chiswick Works, c1916
1998/43651

Royal visit to an LGOC munitions factory, c1916
2013/12119

A support network

The Underground Group produced a staff magazine, TOT (Train Omnibus Tram), to keep troops connected with their families and former colleagues. The organisation also provided practical support for families, including free outings and entertainment, paid for by staff fundraising events.

TOT (Train Omnibus Tram), September 1914

Soldiers on leave join Hounslow bus garage staff on an outing on the Thames at Marlow in Buckinghamshire, August 1916
2013/9824

A whist (card game) tournament at the Central London Railway Institute, Wood Lane, west London, August 1917
2013/9811

PASS RIGHT DOWN THE CAR PLEASE

Every one cannot get a seat at the busy hours but more could get a strap or standing room if the doors were left free from the crush. Think of the others. A door obstructor is a selfish person.

Train delays mean overcrowding.

Electric Railway House, Broadway, Westminster

**Pass right down the car please
George Morrow, 1918**
With full employment and a growing population, overcrowding and delays to services became a serious concern. Etiquette posters like this appealed to travellers' selflessness as well as their patience. The 'crush' was now the norm.

1983/4/815

SOCIAL LIVES

Despite its horror and hardships, war brought full employment and increased income for many. Theatre-land boomed, distracting audiences with light-hearted revues and musicals. The new picture houses showed popular 'movies' and propaganda images from the front. In London's lively Soho area, foreign restaurants became the perfect rendezvous for off-duty soldiers and female war workers. Clubs and dance halls offered an escape for war-weary troops and independent working women.

The Defence of the Realm Act (DORA) was introduced in August 1914 and affected everyone. Censors controlled the flow of information and even pub opening times were limited to curb drunkenness. Food shortages led to rationing, and the growing of vegetables in London parks.

WHY NOT?

Wealthy dames are forming organisations to induce the "lower classes" to practise thrift. Why should not the ladies of the slums follow suit?

Visitor (to President of the Society for inculcating thrift amongst working classes): "Yes mum, I'm Chairman of the Society for advocating Thrift among the the upper classes, an' I jest called in to ask a few questions, to advise you how to spend the week's wages, an' see as you don't throw your money away on unnecessary things!"

'Why Not? Wealthy dames are forming organisations to induce the 'lower classes' to practise thrift', *Railway Review* 1917 Modern Records Centre

A policeman oversees a queue for potatoes in Essex Road, Islington, March 1917 Press Association

Food shortages
German attacks on supply ships, combined with bad harvests, created food shortages. By April 1917 the country was six weeks away from running out of wheat, while potatoes were constantly in short supply. Long queues often ended in disappointment as stores ran out of stock. Voluntary rationing was introduced for staple foods, but prices were increasing rapidly. Cartoons and newspaper articles expressed resentment towards 'profiteers' and those able to pay higher prices.

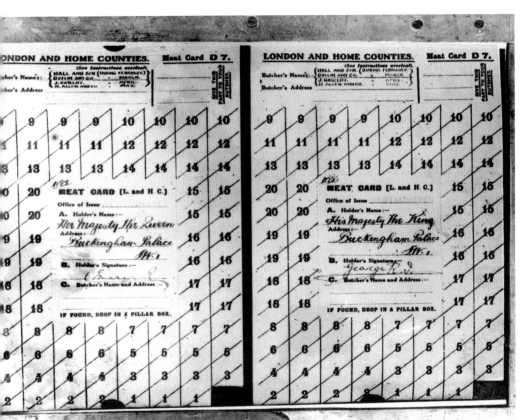

Bus Conductor. "WHERE TO, MADAM?"
Passenger (who has recently given up her car). "THE STORES—QUICKLY AS POSSIBLE. THEN MADAME FIFINETTE; AND I MUST BE AT THE CLUB 4.30 SHARP."

Waste not, want not

Compulsory rationing began in January 1918, to enforce the fair distribution of food. Each person had two ration cards allowing them to buy certain restricted items. Maximum prices were introduced for some foods to stop shop-keepers from taking advantage of shortages. Waste was frowned upon and newspapers expressed disgust at those flouting the rules. It was widely publicised that even the Royal Household was rationed.

Meat ration cards issued to King George V and Queen Mary, 1918
1998/36560

Where to Madam? by J H Dowd, 1917
2013/12533

Chalk Farm to Waterlot Farm

In 1915 Lionel Monckton wrote the popular song Chalk Farm to Camberwell Green for his wife, the theatrical star Gertie Millar, based on a jolly trip on the top of a London bus, and performed in the 'Bric-a-Brac' revue.

The following year Lieutenant EA Mackintosh created a second version with a macabre twist.

Called High Wood to Waterlot Farm, it drew upon the soldier's experience of being wounded and gassed at High Wood on the Somme in August 1916. Mackintosh was killed at Cambrai the following year, aged 24.

Chalk Farm to Camberwell Green
All on a Summer's day
Up we climbed on the motorbus
And it started right away
When we got to the end of the ride
He asked me to go for a walk
But I wasn't Camberwell green
By a very long chalk

LIONEL MONCKTON, 1915

High Wood to Waterlot Farm
All on a summer's day
Up you get to the top of the trench
Though you're sniped at all the way
If you've got a smoke helmet there
You'd best put it on if you could
For the wood down by Waterlot Farm
Is a bloody high wood

LIEUTENANT E A MACKINTOSH MC, 1916

SUNDAY IN TOWN

FOUR INCIDENTS

CHANGING THE GUARD
AT ST JAMES PALACE 11.O.A.M.
BOOK TO DOVER ST OR ST JAMES PARK.

PETTICOAT LANE MARKETS
AT MIDDLESEX STREET
BOOK TO ALDGATE EAST.

THE HOME OF ALL THE CAUSES
AT MARBLE ARCH HYDE PARK
BOOK TO MARBLE ARCH.

CHURCH PARADE
HYDE PARK
BOOK TO HYDE PARK CORNER.

OUT FOR VICTORY.

THE ALLOTMENT HOLDER.
Too old to fight, but doing his bit to beat the U boats.

Out for victory

The Underground Group continued to promote leisure travel in the early months of the war. A stroll in the park remained a popular pastime, but open spaces were also used for the war effort. Crops were grown in Hyde Park and Kensington Gardens, and even in the flower beds outside Buckingham Palace. Sections of Clapham Common were converted to allotments and practice trenches.

Sunday in town, Charles Sharland, 1916
1983/4/745

Out for Victory, 1916
2013/12053

Crop growing in Hyde Park, 1918
Getty Images

'Metro-Land', second edition, 1915

Metro-land was the marketing term applied to the outlying areas of London served by the Metropolitan Railway. The Metro-land guide book first appeared in 1915 and continued to promote life in the suburbs to middle class home-seekers throughout the war.

2000/19748

METRO-LAND

PRICE ONE PENNY.

PALACE Shaftesbury Avenue. W.

1915

"BRIC-À-BRAC."

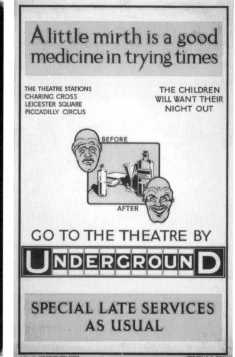

A little mirth is a good medicine in trying times

THE THEATRE STATIONS
CHARING CROSS
LEICESTER SQUARE
PICCADILLY CIRCUS

THE CHILDREN
WILL WANT THEIR
NIGHT OUT

BEFORE

AFTER

GO TO THE THEATRE BY

UNDERGROUND

SPECIAL LATE SERVICES
AS USUAL

Home on leave

As the war dragged on, theatre and cinema remained popular but tastes changed. Comedy plays with topical titles like 'Home on Leave' and 'Billeted' attracted enthusiastic audiences. In 1915 the light-hearted musical revue 'Bric-a-Brac' played at the Palace Theatre for 385 performances in a row.

Programme for 'Bric-A-Brac' at the Palace Theatre, London, 1915.
The City of Westminster Archives Centre

Postcard promoting the play 'Home on Leave' at the Royalty Theatre, Shaftesbury Avenue, 1916
2013/8301

Go to the theatre by Underground,
Artist unknown, 1915
1983/4/619

Wounded soldiers being helped from a B-type bus join a queue outside the Palace Theatre, c1916
1998/70313

Why bother about the Germans invading the country? The Brothers Warbis, 1915
Created in 1915, this poster was one of the last to promote leisure travel in the face of growing fuel shortages. Its light-hearted attitude to the Germans reveals a level of bravado that soon faded as war continued.

1983/4/603

"The Bystander's" Fragments from France

Unappetising

Moments when the Savoy, the Alhambra, and the Piccadilly Grill seem very far away (the offensive starts in half an hour)

Soho nights

Soho's foreign restaurants, cafes and patisseries were popular with workers from Whitehall's expanded wartime government ministries. There were also around 200 nightclubs in Soho alone. Establishment figures such as the Bishop of London complained that most were 'disreputable'.

A moral panic whipped up by the press suggested that female munitions workers were 'drinking away their over-generous allowances' and young troops were succumbing to the evils of drink, drugs and prostitution. The Defence of the Realm Act (DORA) restricted the sale of alcohol.

Soldiers miss famous West End entertainments in this typical Bruce Bairnsfather cartoon, 1917
2013/12123

Women waving goodbye to troops at Victoria Station, January 1915
Getty Images

Young couples on the dance floor at Murray's Club, a fashionable Soho venue, 1919
Getty Images

Charlie Chaplin cartoon, Punch, 1915

Charlie Chaplin made his film debut in 1914 and by the end of the war he was a star. However, the actor was heavily criticised in the newspapers for not joining the army and regarded by many as a shirker.

© Punch Limited

Near-sighted Old Lady (a keen Recruiter). "NOW LOOK AT THAT YOUNG FELLOW. A COUPLE OF MONTHS IN THE ARMY WOULD MAKE A NEW MAN OF HIM!"

THE BUSES GO TO WAR

The First World War involved fighting on land, sea and in the air, worldwide. In Europe the war was fought on several fronts. Germany and her allies fought Russia on the Eastern Front, and Britain and France in the west. The Western Front ran from the North Sea through northern Belgium and France, to the border with Switzerland. This was the first war to use motorised transport alongside horses. The British Army did not have enough of its own vehicles, so to move troops quickly over one thousand buses were transferred from London's streets to the Western Front.

LONDON

ENGLAND

ENGLISH
CHANNEL

BRUSSELS

BELGIUM

GERMANY

LUXEMBOURG

FRANCE

PARIS

MAP KEY

▪▪▪▪▪ Frontline 1914

——— Frontline 1918

**London buses in Boulogne,
northern France, August 1914**
The first buses sent to war were initially
part of the Royal Naval Division. Here,
the drivers wear waterproof capes and
protect their cabs from the rain using
tarpaulins marked with the London
General Omnibus Company initials.

1998/83862

OFF TO THE FRONT

London buses played a vital role in supporting Britain and her allies during the war. From August 1914, several hundred buses were sent to support the British Army in France and Belgium. Many were driven by the same men who had driven them through London's streets, while working for the London General Omnibus Company (LGOC).

As the war continued, the buses became part of a highly organised transport network serving the Western Front. Some were taken as far away as Egypt as war spread around the world.

London bus carrying troops in Ghent, Belgium, 1914

The first London buses to go to war as troop transport were deployed rapidly, keeping their blue London MET (Metropolitan Electric Tramways) livery. In October 1914, they played a vital role in rescuing soldiers and civilians from the invading German Army during the siege of Antwerp in Belgium.

1998/84914

British troops and two London buses on the quayside at Ostend, Belgium, 1914

British troops look on as wounded soldiers are unloaded from a London bus, still carrying its last advertisements. Supplies are loaded onto a nearby lorry converted from an LGOC bus.

The first British soldiers sent to the Western Front were part of the British Expeditionary Force (BEF). These men were 'regular' soldiers, for whom the army was their occupation. Most were killed or wounded in the first few months of the war.

In September 1914, the British government made an emergency request for 75 buses and their drivers to support the defence of the coastal ports of Boulogne, Calais, Dunkirk, and Ostend, as well as some areas further inland.

1998/84320 ←

Captured buses

Of the first 75 buses sent to war in August 1914, more than 20, including D219 see here in Bruges, Belgium, were either captured by German forces or damaged beyond repair.

1998/88525
1998/36089

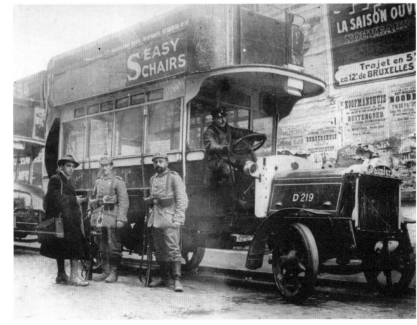

THE ARMY SERVICE CORPS

THE MILITARY TRAIN AND ITS WORK

AT one time the Army Service Corps was known unofficially as "The Muck Train," and officially as "The Military Train." After the Crimean War, however, its existence as the Military Train practically ceased, and it was remodelled on its present lines within comparatively recent years. In the table

and with full dress a cloth-covered helmet is worn. On active service, however, everybody wears khaki. Those of its members now in the field are mostly Reservists, as enlistment is only for a short period "with the colours." The term "colours," by the way, is a misnomer, for the Army Service Corps, like the Artillery and Engineers, does not carry "colours."

BRITISH TRANSPORT TRAIN ON THE MARCH NEAR MONS. Copyright.
From a photograph taken by an officer at the front.

of precedence it comes just after the West India Regiment. The corps' motto is "Nil sine labore." This is a very appropriate one, for the A.S.C. (as it is always known) has an immense amount of work to do, especially at a time like the present, when the British troops are in the field. The uniform of the corps is blue with white "facings."

The Army Service Corps is divided into horse transport companies, mechanical transport companies, supply companies and remount companies, and detachments from these serve pretty nearly everywhere except in India. The mechanical transport companies work with motor lorries and traction engines, and are of special value when there is a

Army Service Corps

The Army Service Corps (ASC) supplied food, tents, baggage, ammunition and equipment to the entire British Army. In October 1914 it also took over responsibility for London's buses on the Western Front. The ASC buses transported soldiers to and from battle, as well as all of the supplies needed for war. Although its men were exposed to the threat of attack, many fighting troops considered them to have an easy life, nicknaming them Ally Sloper's Cavalry after a lazy, blustering Victorian cartoon character.

'The Army Service Corps', *Army & Navy* magazine, October 1914, 2013/11809

Typical army base camp served by the ASC, *Navy and Army* magazine, October 1914. 2013/11806

Preparing for the front

The ASC took over a large workhouse for the poor in Grove Park, south London. It was here that London buses were gathered before travelling to France and Belgium. London bus drivers taught new ASC recruits how to drive and maintain vehicles from January 1915 onwards. As space was limited, surrounding streets were used for vehicle preparation and repairs. Driver training also took place at the army camp in Osterley Park, west London.

Postcards of Grove Park Depot and surrounding area, 1915
Courtesy of the Michael Young Collection

'Three hundred of us (LGOC drivers) volunteered, put into Army uniform overnight, within a week we were out in France.'
GEORGE GWYNN, LGOC BUS DRIVER ON THE WESTERN FRONT, INTERVIEWED BY LONDON TRANSPORT MUSEUM IN 1985.

Instructors on war
service, Osterley Park,
west London, c1916
Courtesy of the Michael
Young Collection ←

Army Service Corps (ASC) drivers receive training on engine maintenance from an LGOC instructor, London, 1915 1998/36584

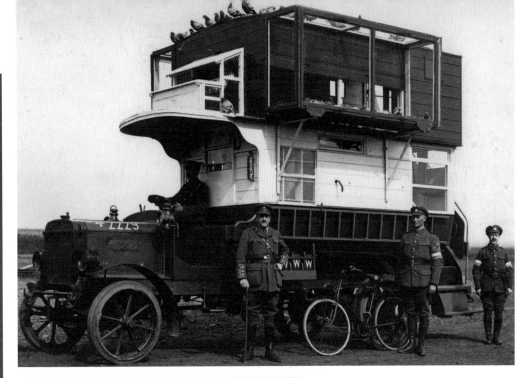

ONE BUS, MANY USES

The B-type bus was surprisingly easy to adapt for military use. Following traditional coach-building techniques, London buses were formed by placing a wood and glass body onto a separate metal frame or chassis.

Many of the buses were used to carry troops into battle. However, the London bus chassis were versatile and could be adapted into a range of specialised vehicles, from ambulances and messenger-pigeon lofts to anti-aircraft gun carriages and freight lorries.

Sending messages
One of the most reliable forms of secret communication in warfare was to attach messages to specially-trained homing pigeons, which could travel unnoticed through the air. The birds were taken to battle areas where they were released to fly back to their 'homes' behind the front line, which included specially converted London buses. By the end of 1916, there were six pigeon buses and a further six were ordered in 1917.

1999/20005

Wheels of war
The robust B-type bus chassis was very versatile. Anti-aircraft guns were mounted to bus chassis to provide mobile artillery and bus B752 was even converted into an armoured patrol car for the Royal Navy.

Armoured patrol car, Belgium, 1914
2013/12209

Anti-aircraft guns mounted on bus chassis, Western Front, c1915. 1998/49160

'On returning from a march we had a great surprise… we found several Frenchmen, acting under orders, sawing away the upper parts of the buses… turning them into lorries.'

EDWARD DARBY, LGOC DRIVER, INTERVIEWED BY LONDON TRANSPORT MUSEUM IN 1984

LA GUERRE DANS LE NORD
2 BÉTHUNE — Les Autobus de Londres

Buses as ambulances

Buses helped wounded soldiers to safety. Casualties were transferred by bus to stationary hospitals for recuperation, such as the important casualty station at Bethune, northern France, before returning to the trenches or being discharged and returning home.

London buses, Bethune, northern France, c1915
Courtesy of the Michael Young Collection   ↑

Walking wounded soldiers board an LGOC bus converted into an ambulance on the Western Front, 1914-18
1998/38988   ←

Model of B-type motor bus

London buses sent to France with the Army Service Corps were repainted in khaki camouflage and had their windows boarded over.

1:16 scale.
1992/229

THE ROAD TO THE TRENCHES

By Christmas 1914, the war had become a static fight between two opposing armies. To provide protection against attack without giving up hard-won territory, both sides dug networks of trenches in which they lived, fought and died. Behind the front line, reserve trenches allowed waiting soldiers and supplies to move to the Front. Behind these were facilities supplied by the Army Service Corps (ASC), including food preparation and ammunition stores.

By autumn 1915, five ASC units were operating as Auxiliary Omnibus Companies at the Front, along with two further companies of lorries. The seven companies had bases and workshops across northern France. A year later, all available vehicles were grouped together at the 'Auxiliary Omnibus Park' in St. Valery sur Somme, on the French coast.

Centralised operations meant that buses could be organised at short notice. The 650 buses operated a regular service behind the front lines, with convoys of 70 or 80 vehicles routinely making nightly troop transport movements.

In convoy

The buses travelled in columns that could exceed 100 vehicles, at only about eight miles per hour to ensure there were no stragglers. Troop movements at the front usually took place under cover of darkness to avoid detection by the enemy.

Night convoy of French lorries, L'Illustration, March 1916
2013/11800   ↖

A convoy of London buses transports Indian troops at the Front, 1915.
1998/36644   ←

Troops 'embussing', Western Front, c1917

A column of buses could be in position and ready to move troops to or from the front line within an hour of receiving orders. Whole divisions (20,000 men) could be 'embussed' (boarded) in just half an hour. In 1917 alone, 1.2 million men were carried nearly 3 million miles.

1998/39220

Bus driver Walter John Cornell, c1914

Cornell, seen here in ASC uniform, had been a bus driver based at Cricklewood Garage in north London. At the outbreak of war, he was sent to France to drive troops to and from the Front. Conditions were tough as the drivers' cabs were exposed to the elements. Cornell's goggles offered little protection from the elements.

2004/8008

'… we were actually on the road 18 hours per day…
We had hardly time to wash and had most of our
meals while the bus was on the run.'

WILLIAM MAHONEY, ASC BUS DRIVER 1916-17

Women in supporting roles

While women were not allowed to join the fighting troops, many worked in important roles to support the Allied war effort in France and Belgium. Some became ambulance drivers or nurses, caring for the wounded and transporting them to safety.

1998/42862

Soldiers posing by a B-type bus, Western Front, 1914-15

Men from many parts of the British Empire came together to fight, and they rode together on the London buses as comrades. This photograph shows Sikh troops from India on the upper deck. It was taken during the early part of the war, before the windows were boarded up for protection. The word 'comrades' appears on the side of the bus.

1998/42862 ↙

Trench on the Western Front, 1915-18

A soldier stands in a narrow mud-walled trench. Soldiers sometimes labelled the trenches with London street names to aid navigation.

1998/51100 →

Detailed instructions

Where possible, the ASC operated regular deliveries of food for men and horses, as well as fuel, ammunition and the all-important post from home to the front lines. Every movement was carefully described in written orders and shown on detailed diagrams.

Traffic map, 18th Divisional Mechanical Transport, 1918.
The Royal Logistic Corps Museum →

Instructions to Private Hastie, ASC, 1918
The Royal Logistic Corps Museum →

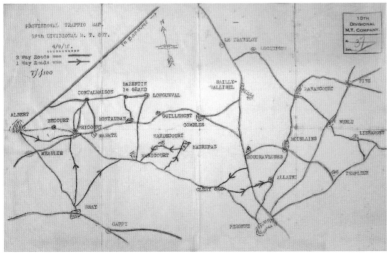

REST AND RELAXATION

Men in the armed services developed their own culture and habits. Life in the trenches often saw troops facing long periods of inactivity, punctuated by frightening episodes under fire. To pass the time when not on duty, soldiers might read, write letters home or even sketch scenes from the Front or write poetry.

When not actively working around combat areas, bus drivers were given a base depot behind the front lines where they could relax.

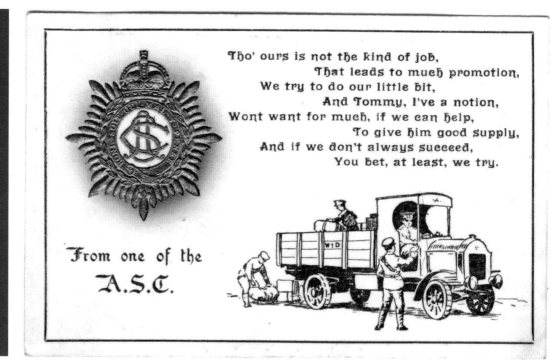

Army Service Corps postcard, c1915
Troops at the Western Front included many young men who had never been away from home before. Postcard manufacturers soon saw an opportunity to sell products to help troops keep in touch with relatives and sweethearts back home.

The Royal Logistic Corps Museum

Sweetheart brooch and ring, c1916
To occupy themselves during periods of inactivity, men made presents for wives and girlfriends from surplus materials such as shell cases and cap badges. These objects, called 'sweethearts', could also be purchased as ready-made items from towns in France and Belgium.

The Royal Logistic Corps Museum

YMCA huts

The Young Men's Christian Association (YMCA) ran rest facilities for troops behind the front lines, including one sponsored by LGOC as a recreation and rest hut for bus drivers. Described grandly as 'a Winter Garden and Theatre', the facility was located in Rouen, northern France, around 90 miles from the fighting front. It offered men a chance to relax, catch up on home news and buy food not available at the front line. Alongside the hut were living quarters for vehicle operators and mechanics. Actress Lena Ashwell created 25 acting groups to entertain the troops and civilian workers in France. One of her groups visited a make-shift theatre at the LGOC YMCA Hut in 1915, which was seen by 1,000 people. Some servicemen created their own entertainment, putting on theatrical and musical productions.

Army Service Corps members watch actress Lena Ashwell, at the YMCA hut in Rouen, northern France, 1915. TOT (Train Omnibus Tram) staff magazine, October 1915

YMCA huts, Rouen, northern France, c1915 Cadbury Research Library: Special Collections, The University of Birmingham

Army Service Corps theatre production, France 1917 2004/8997

AUGUST BANK HOLIDAY SPORTS AT THE T.O.T HUT, ROUEN, FRANCE (BASE FOR MECHANICAL TRANSPORT).

LONDON MEMORIES

LONDON MEMORIES

DENHAM WITH THE COMPLIMENTS OF THE UNDERGROUND RYS.

WIMBLEDON COMMON WITH THE COMPLIMENTS OF THE UNDERGROUND RYS.

London Memories – Denham, Emilio Tafani, 1918
1983/4/713

London Memories – Wimbledon Common, Emilio Tafani, 1918
1999/43242

London Memories

Before the war, the Underground Group had developed a reputation for commissioning successful advertising posters. Colourful designs presented London in a new light, encouraging people to take trips to the countryside, theatre or the zoo. As the war dragged on it became inappropriate to promote non-essential leisure travel. Instead, propaganda posters for display at home and abroad were commissioned.

Four posters, titled 'London Memories', were sent to troops fighting on the Western Front. The posters were displayed in army billets to raise morale and to remind soldiers of home.

London Memories – Hampstead, Fred Taylor, 1918
1983/4/720

London Memories – Kew Gardens, Fred Taylor, 1918
1983/4/717

CONFLICTS AND DESTINATIONS

As war progressed, army units became associated with the battles in which they had fought. Some buses were given their own roll of honour showing the battles at which they had been present. Many buses were damaged or destroyed in the conflict. Of the 1,185 buses taken to war, only 230 would return to London.

Army Corps drivers in front of a B-type bus, Western Front, 1915
Though they were repainted, some buses kept their original destination boards, which were sometimes adapted to raise morale. The destination board here indicates Victoria Station, while the words 'To Berlin' have been added below. London buses did not go as far as Berlin, but some did go as far as the German city of Cologne in 1919.

1998/36618

'Most of the buses have been christened with chalk, with the favourite names of wives or sweethearts, with the addition of "take your tickets for Berlin."'

PRIVATE W LUFFRUM, ARMY VETINARY CORPS, IN TOT (TRAIN OMNIBUS TRAM) STAFF MAGAZINE, AUGUST 1915

Buses taking troops into battle at Armentières, northern France, October 1914

The battle of Armentières took place early in the war. London buses took troops towards the front line. This new wartime sight was commemorated in images such as this one.

2013/12311

'Ole Bill' plate, 1920

London buses were present at most of the major conflicts along the Western Front. This plate was originally attached to bus B43, later known as 'Ole Bill'. It shows a list of five major battle locations at which London buses served.

1999/27354

A Sudden Strike Fortunino Matania, c1915

Matania's painting focuses on a London bus caught in front line fighting. Despite the drama of the image, in reality buses were rarely at the heart of battle, usually only taking troops as far as the reserve trenches.

The Royal Logistic Corps Museum

Servicemen stand by an adapted American vehicle, Belgium, c1918

Inevitably, vehicles became damaged in use. To maintain the number of buses available for war service, surplus wooden bus bodies could be mounted onto lorry chassis to create new vehicles. Here a B-type body is mounted on an American Locomobile lorry chassis.

Courtesy of the Michael Young Collection

'We started our engines, our hearts in our mouths. Bang! Crash!! Nearly on us. Nine men killed and 14 wounded only 50 yards away. My engine would not start so there we had to stay and repair it, shells pouring around us.'

WILLIAM MAHONEY, ASC BUS DRIVER 1916-17

Steering wheel with First World War inscriptions

This steering wheel is an example of 'trench art', a term describing decorative items made by soldiers, prisoners of war or civilians during conflict. Trench art is often made from found items related to war.

The wheel has been marked with some of the notable battles in which London buses participated as well as references to army life and slang, and reminders of home. Maconochie was a thin stew of meat, sliced turnips, carrots and potatoes, often served cold to troops. Jack Johnson was an African-American boxer, heavyweight champion of the world between 1908 and 1915. His name was applied to the impact of a large German artillery shell. 'Blighty', was a sentimental reference to Britain, but the term was also used for a small injury that would enable men to return home for treatment.

2013/10111

'We went into the firing line 1,000 strong, and when roll was called on Saturday morning there were only 75 men answered their names… It was not war it was pure murder.'

PRIVATE F LART, TOT (TRAIN OMNIBUS TRAM)
STAFF MAGAZINE, MAY 1915

Driver Alfred Chouffot with Distinguished Service Medal, 1914

Alfred Chouffot was one of the first London bus men to be awarded the Distinguished Service Medal, for his work overseeing buses in the retreat from Antwerp in 1914. Other Auxiliary Omnibus Company men won many more awards, including 21 Military Medals for their work in spring 1918 when German forces mounted a major offensive against the British and French.

TOT (Train Omnibus Tram) staff magazine, February 1916

Sergeant Grigg, Private Bowman and Lance Corporal Sadler, prisoners of war, 1916

Troops on both sides were captured and taken as prisoners of war. Conditions in prison camps were mixed, but some men found the opportunity to have photographs taken to send home with news of their survival. Several of these were published in the staff magazine.

TOT (Train Omnibus Tram) staff magazine, July 1916

London Transport artist Walter Spradbery – a pacifist at the Front

Civilians who refused to fight on grounds of conscience were known as conscientious objectors (COs). Some COs accepted auxiliary roles which avoided direct conflict. Some were imprisoned or tried for desertion on refusing conscription.

Artist Walter Spradbery, who produced 90 posters for London Transport between 1912 and 1945, was a lifelong pacifist who volunteered for the non-combatant Royal Army Medical Corps ambulance service. He painted scenes of life at the front, and won a Distinguished Conduct Medal for rescuing wounded infantrymen whilst under fire in 1918.

Stretcher bearers passing a bombed factory, France
Walter Spradbery, August 1918
Image courtesy of Wellcome Library

Carrying the wounded at Buire-sur-Corbie, France
Walter Spradbery, August 1918
Image courtesy of Wellcome Library

Convoy of buses to take troops to battle, Cassel, France, 8 August 1917
Casualties were high throughout the war and the fighting units needed a constant supply of men. Reinforcements were transported from rest areas towards the battle locations by bus. Here, a long convoy waits for orders, as the Battle of Passchendaele in Belgium rages just 25 miles to the east.

1998/40302

Cheering troops on the top decks of buses, Arras, France, April 1917
Buses took men into battle, and they brought the survivors away from the front lines for respite. Here troops cheer for the camera in the town square at Arras, northern France, having returned from fighting in nearby Monchy-le-Preux.

1998/46269

DETROIT DAILY NEWS

12 NOVEMBER 1918

WAR OVER
GERMANS
SIGN TRUCE

After four years of conflict, a succession of major Allied offensives in September and October 1918 broke the stalemate. Newly-arrived American troops took part in the fighting, the USA having joined the Allies the previous year.

Negotiations for a cease-fire, or armistice, started on 5 November, and the German Kaiser abdicated within days. The armistice was signed at 5am on 11 November 1918. During the four years of war, nearly 9 million soldiers and 7 million civilians were killed.

PEACE AT LAST

At 11am on 11 November 1918, hostilities ended and German troops started to withdraw from France and Belgium. Life in London did not improve in the short term and rationing continued until 1920. Many people celebrated victory, while others were simply relieved that the fighting was over. A devastating influenza pandemic claimed millions more lives. Wounded, disabled and shell-shocked troops started to come home. Women employed as 'substitutes' gave their jobs up to returning soldiers, but many men were left unfit and unable to work.

POST WAR LONDON

As London returned to peacetime life, public transport struggled to cope with continuing shortages and economic difficulties. Some buses limped home from the front, but few were fit to go back into civilian service. Carefully worded Underground posters were issued to justify rising ticket prices in the face of rampant post-war inflation and unemployment.

Social unrest resumed across the country. Changes in law tripled the size of the electorate for the December 1918 election, including all men over 21 and married or property-owning women over 30.

Opposing views
London celebrated, but the devastation of war led many returning troops to demand a better world afterwards.

Daily Mirror, 12 November 1918
2013/8379

Cartoon from the Railway Review, 1918
Modern Records Centre

ALLIES' DRASTIC ARMISTICE TERMS TO HUNS

The Daily Mirror

CERTIFIED CIRCULATION LARGER THAN THAT OF ANY OTHER DAILY PICTURE PAPER

No. 4,696.   Registered at the G.P.O. as a Newspaper.   TUESDAY, NOVEMBER 12, 1918   One Penny.

HOW LONDON HAILED THE END OF WAR

The King and Queen appeared on the balcony at Buckingham Palace to acknowledge the cheers of the crowd that gathered to congratulate their Majesties on the victory.

Home on short leave, but now safe for always from the dangers of Hun bullet and steel.

How news of the armistice signature came over the wire to the newspaper offices. A facsimile of it as automatically printed on the tape machine. The cheers which greeted it were the first to be raised.

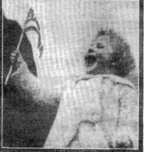

"Now entitled to rejoice" and doing it. Daddy has beaten the Huns and is coming home.

Nothing gave greater satisfaction to all of us than the news that the cessation of hostilities found the British armies once more in possession of Mons, where the immortal

An historic message as it came over the wire. It is dramatic that the last British war communiqué should proclaim our forces at Mons.

"Contemptibles" first taught the Huns what British valour and steadfastness could do. They left the town as defenders of a forlorn hope; they re-entered it conquerors indeed.

Women out

As discharged soldiers returned to civilian life their employment was considered a priority. Most female transport workers had to give up their jobs to allow men back into the workforce. In November 1919, the last female bus conductor, Ellen Bulfield, was photographed ceremoniously handing her job over to a male colleague.

London Underground Railways and the LGOC organised a 'farewell social gathering' for female war workers. All the women were presented with a certificate of service. Conductor Florence Cordell reflected that, 'if I'd have been a single girl... I would have liked to have stopped on.'

Photograph of LGOC farewell social gathering,
October 1919
1998/43329

LGOC certificate of service issued to
Ellen Bulfield, 1919
2001/53590

Photograph of female bus conductor
Ellen Bulfield, 1919
2001/56628

'We knew we were only there for the duration... when the men came back we were given our cards, and that was that.'

ANNE PARKER, LGOC BUS CONDUCTOR, INTERVIEWED
BY LONDON TRANSPORT MUSEUM IN 1990

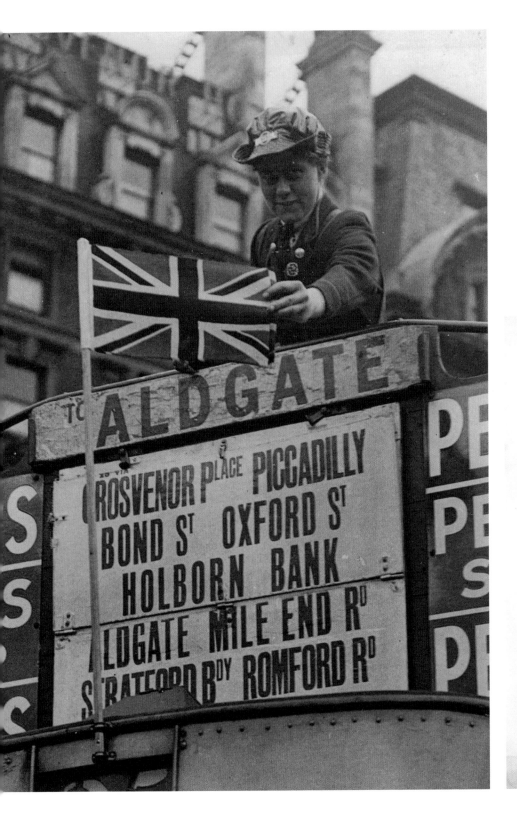

Peace or victory?

The first nationwide commemoration of the war on 19 July 1919 was called Peace Day. It included a massed choir in Hyde Park singing a 'Chorus of Peace and Thanksgiving'. By contrast, a march of 15,000 servicemen through London was styled as a 'Victory Parade', and led by Allied commanders. In Whitehall, the Cenotaph, a new monument dedicated to 'The Glorious Dead' was unveiled.

TOT Victory Day, June 1919
1998/36862

Peace Day notice, July 1919
1983/4/983

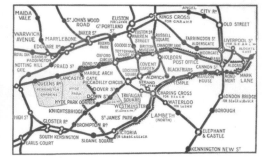

UNDERGROUND

PEACE DAY. JULY 19th

MAP OF ILLUMINATION AREA

(The Area inside the Red Line will be closed to Motor-Bus traffic after 8 p.m.)

TIMES OF LAST TRAINS.

District Railway.		Bakerloo Line.	
FROM CHARING CROSS TO		FROM CHARING CROSS TO	
EALING	12 46 a.m.	QUEEN'S PARK	12 57 a.m.
UXBRIDGE	11 30 a.m.	WATFORD	11 25 p.m.
HOUNSLOW	12 24 a.m.	ELEPHANT & CASTLE	1 3 a.m.
RICHMOND	11 53 p.m.		
ACTON	1 8 a.m.	**Piccadilly Line.**	
PUTNEY	1 8 a.m.		
WIMBLEDON	12 36 a.m.	FROM PICCADILLY CIRCUS TO	
EAST HAM	12 36 a.m.	FINSBURY PARK	1 0 a.m.
BARKING	12 19 a.m.	HAMMERSMITH	1 3 a.m.

Hampstead Line.		Central London Railway.	
FROM CHARING CROSS TO		FROM OXFORD CIRCUS TO	
GOLDERS GREEN	1 0 a.m.	LIVERPOOL STREET	12 49 a.m.
HIGHGATE	1 0 a.m.	WOOD LANE	1 10 a.m.

City & South London Railway.	
FROM BANK TO	
CLAPHAM COMMON	11 48 p.m.
EUSTON	11 28 p.m.

Battered survivors

Less than one quarter of the 1,185 buses sent overseas by the government returned to London. These battered survivors were judged 'substandard' for conveying regular passengers, but shortages of materials to build new vehicles meant that some were used in May 1919 as basic 'Traffic Emergency' buses. They were re-painted in the khaki of the battlefields, to indicate they were substandard, with the General logo in white on the side. In addition, the Metropolitan Police regulations for bus vehicles were relaxed in 1919, allowing the LGOC to relicense pre-war bus chassis equipped with simple wooden lorry bodies, like this one at Victoria Station.

LGOC workers examine a B-type bus returned from the front, December 1919
1998/87303

Lorry-bus at Victoria Station, central London, 1919
1998/75373

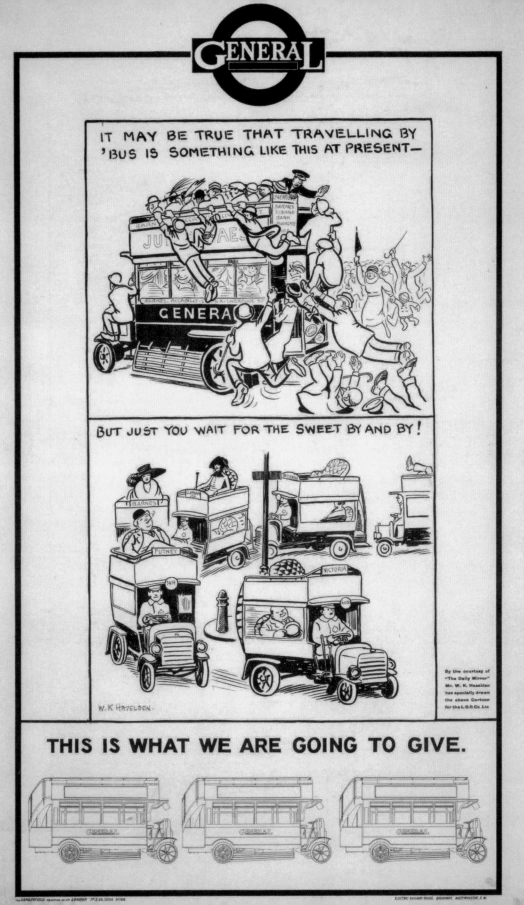

Underground Group posters in the years after the First World War presented a variety of messages about the service. They acknowledged continuing problems such as overcrowding but promised a better future.

This is what we are going to give. William Kerridge Haselden, 1920
1983/4/887

COMMEMORATION

The First World War brought death and devastation on an unprecedented scale. Millions of lives had been lost and millions more were affected by injury and bereavement. People looked for ways to remember and honour the dead. The Cenotaph was unveiled on Whitehall in central London as the national war memorial and has become a focus for remembrance ever since.

Like many other industries and communities, London's transport workers established memorials to their dead in garages, stations and offices.

Remembrance Day

The 1920 Remembrance Day was a carefully planned event. A formal military parade included B-type bus B43 driving past the newly unveiled Cenotaph in Whitehall. LGOC veterans were the only civilian unit included in the parade, marching alongside the bus. With its combination of war and home front service, the B-type symbolised both military and civilian efforts.

Philip Bowden, an LGOC employee who had fought during the war, was chosen to lay the company wreath at the Cenotaph. Bowden had been awarded the Military Medal for his bravery.

LGOC wreath, 1920
2009/54

LGOC employee Philip Bowden, 1918
2009/79

Armistice Day parade, 1923
2007/10528 ←

13 Clifton Rd.
Sth Norwood

Thursday.   *Dec 7 '16*

Dear Sid,

*Dear little Bertha has
gone. She died today at 5
o-clock. But her bright little
life has not been wasted &
she leaves behind the happiest
of memories. She has gone to
heaven & left to us an angel
which will live in our dreams
& memories for ever. Ta-ta keep
fit.*

*Your affectionate.
brother
Joe.*

Philip Bowden (1898–1981)

Philip Bowden started work in the LGOC accounts office in 1912, aged just 14. At 17, he joined the Royal Field Artillery and was sent to fight in France and Belgium. Like many young men, Bowden lied about his age when he joined up.

These objects were donated by his daughter Jean in 2008 to make sure he was not forgotten.

Philip Bowden in the uniform of the Royal Field Artillery, 1915
2009/77

Army recruitment form for Philip Bowden, 1915
2009/50

Two letters

On 7 December 1916, Joe Bowden wrote to tell his brother that his favourite little sister Bertha had died that day.

A year later, Bowden's family received a form letter from the war department completed three weeks after he was injured in a gas attack. The attack affected his eyesight, but he was not discharged from service.

Letter from Joe Bowden, 7 December 1916
2008/5825

Notification of injury sent to Philip Bowden's parents, 3 January 1918
2009/49

Three medals

Having recovered from his injuries, Bowden was once more under enemy fire in 1918. He was awarded the Military Medal for carrying a wounded colleague to safety. The award made the local news, with Bowden reported as saying 'it was only what any of the boys would do'.

Military Medal, 1919
2008/5819

Great War Medal, 1919
2008/5821

Victory War Medal, 1919
2008/5822

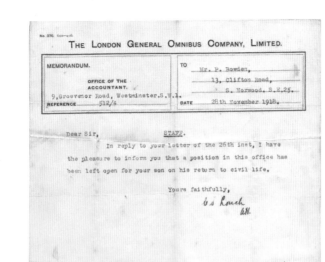

Back to work

Bowden and his family were anxious about his job when the war ended. The LGOC sent this letter to his father shortly after the Armistice to reassure them his job remained open for his return. Bowden continued working for the LGOC, later London Transport, until he retired in 1958.

Letter from the LGOC, 1918
2009/76

Philip Bowden, c1958
2009/81

Family photographs carried by Philip Bowden during the war, c1915

Bowden was the eldest of ten children and carried 59 small photographs of his parents, siblings and their house with him to France. Most of them are included here. His daughter, Jean Bowden, imagined her father 'sitting in a wet cold trench looking at the family pictures taken in happier times'.

2009/83

'They sleep beneath those countless crosses which stud the fields of France, Flanders, Gallipoli, Mesopotamia, Palestine and Macedonia.'

TOT (TRAIN OMNIBUS TRAM),
STAFF MAGAZINE DECEMBER, 1919

A B-type bus St Eloi, Belgium, 1914
This B-type bus was abandoned in Belgium, wrecked by shell-fire two weeks after leaving London. It gave its name to the nearby Bus House Cemetery at St Eloi, where 206 Allied soldiers are now buried.

1998/84919

London Transport Old Comrades Association, London, c2009
The role of London's transport companies during wartime is commemorated annually. Members of London Transport Old Comrades Association have marched alongside other veterans at the Remembrance Day parade since 1920.

2010/4462

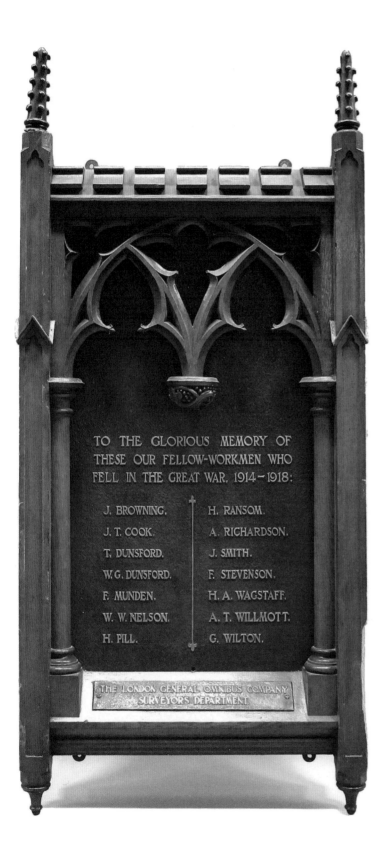

Remembering friends

A total of 1,429 Underground Group employees were lost in action, never to return to the normal rhythm and progress of their lives. They were remembered by their fellow workers who named them individually in plaques and memorials unveiled in depots and garages across the city.

Surveyor's Department of the London General Omnibus Company memorial plaque, c1920
1996/2976

Audit Office of the Underground Group memorial plaque, c1919
1997/13161

Unveiling the memorial at Willesden Bus Garage commemorating 55 workers who died in the First World War, 10 November 1920
1998/43613

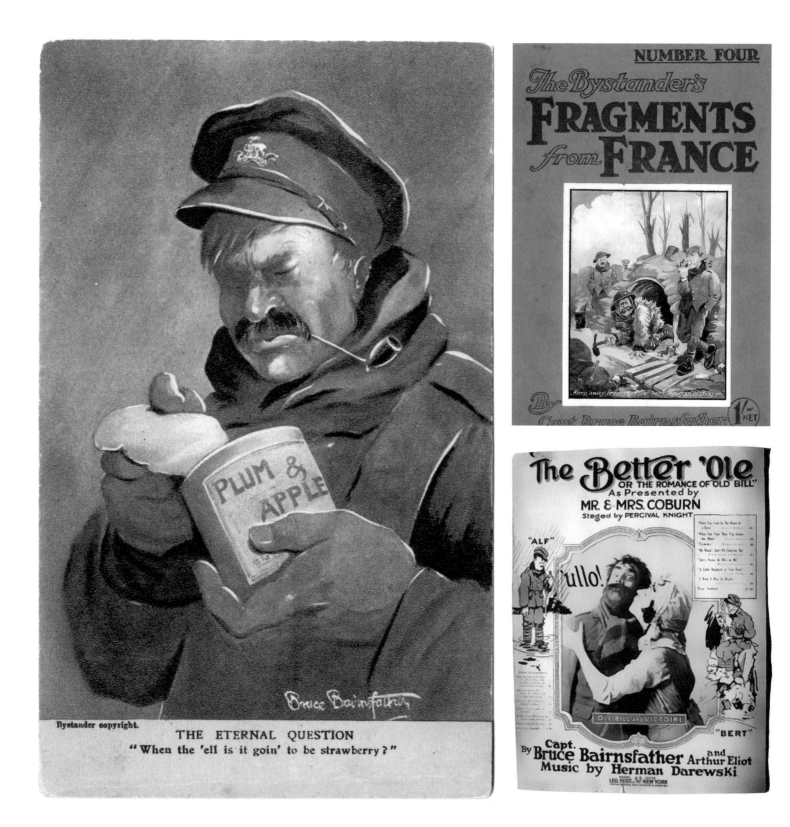

Fragments from France

Bruce Bairnsfather created the cartoon character of 'Ole Bill', while serving as a machine-gun officer in France in 1915. Bairnsfather was injured and returned to Britain, where his humorous sketches soon appeared in 'The Bystander' magazine. The first collection of illustrations in the series 'Fragments from France' sold 260,000 copies.

'Ole Bill' became instantly recognisable and his face was reproduced on popular merchandise. The name refers to a shell hole or 'Ole. Books, plays and films were created around the character. By representing the everyday life of those sent to fight, Bairnsfather's irreverent cartoons captured the absurdity of war.

The Eternal Question, Bruce Bairnsfather, 1915
2013/8312

Song sheet, The Better 'Ole, 1917 2013/12151

Fragments from France, Bruce Bairnsfather, 1917
Private collection

'Ole Bill' the B-type bus

Bus B43 was built in 1911 and later used to transport troops in France and Belgium during the war. In 1919, it arrived back battered and war worn, returning to work on the streets of London the same year.

On 11 November 1920, Bus B43 was driven in the Armistice Day Parade. The bus was nicknamed 'Ole Bill' and adorned with a radiator mascot and nameplate. An empty shell casing was fixed above the dashboard and in this way the bus became a symbol of the wartime efforts of the men and women of the LGOC. It was given a new body and passed to the Old Comrades Association in 1924.

King George V raises his hat to ASC veterans on B43 at Buckingham Palace, February 1920
1998/64651

'Ole Bill' bus B43 flanked by standard bearers in the Armistice Day parade, 1920
1998/75682

Airfix model kit, 1960s

Over time, the name 'Ole Bill' became synonymous with all B-type buses and was often corrupted to 'Old Bill'. This Airfix model of a wartime B-type bus was manufactured in the 1960s.

2013/8609

The last days of the B-type

After the war, some B-type buses were sold off to operators as far afield as Australia, while others continued to serve London until 1926. When their chassis were scrapped, bodies were sometimes saved and survived as sheds, like this one drawn by Eric Ravilious in 1934.

Eric Ravilious, No.29 Bus, c1934
©Towner, Eastbourne

Ex-LGOC B-type operated by Bender's Bus Lines, Australia, 1922-3
Mike Sutcliffe Collection

A NEW LONDON

London and its public transport
emerged from post-war depression
to flourish in the 1920s. The
number of surviving B-type buses
in service dwindled, and were soon
outnumbered and outclassed by
a range of new, bigger and more
powerful buses. Pre-war plans for
Underground expansion were also
revived with government assistance.
Tube lines reached out to Edgware
in the north in 1924, and Morden in
the south in 1926.

NS-type bus in Piccadilly Circus, 1929
Technological advances in bus design
came quickly during the 1920s. By the
end of the decade, new buses were fitted
with covered tops and pneumatic tyres as
standard.

1998/85415

The Strand, central London, packed with buses, 1923
1999/7689

L.G.O.C. Motor Omnibus Milestones.

B. Type
on service Oct. 1910.

K. Type
on service Aug. 1919.

S. Type
on service Dec. 1920.

N.S. Type
on service May. 1923.

Bus evolution

The basic chassis of London's new bus, known as the K-type, had been developed by LGOC engineers in 1914, but progress was halted due to the war. Bus production resumed in 1919. The K-type's longer and wider body, developed at Chiswick Works, provided ten more seats than the B-type.

It was followed quickly by the S-type and the NS-type, which would later develop to become the first bus to have a covered top deck and pneumatic rather than solid tyres.

Aerial view of the LGOC's Chiswick Works, about 1921
2005-568

Bus development, from 1910 to 1923
1998-81251

Bus conductor, Elijah Albert Cox, 1920
By the time Elijah Cox was commissioned to produce a series of posters depicting London Characters in 1920, the figure of the male bus conductor was firmly re-established. Women did not return to work on the buses until the Second World War.

1983/4/1008

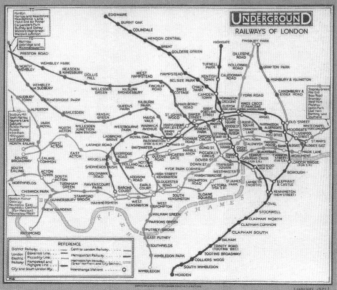

Expansion and co-ordination

A bigger network of extended bus routes fed the Underground extensions into the suburbs in the 1920s. Speculative private builders soon filled in the open land around the built-up areas of the city.

New houses on Elliot Road, Hendon, north London, 1924
1998/17187

Pocket Underground map by Fred Stingemore, 1927
1991/242

Omnibus services from Edgware Station, 1929
2006/3585 part 283

Piccadilly forever

Generations of red buses have carried passengers on the streets of London since the 1920s, and Piccadilly Circus remains one of the Capital's great focal points for tourists and Londoners alike.

Innovation in motor bus design which began with the B-type has continued for over 100 years.

Photograph by Marden Smith, 2014